D1439066

MEIN RANT

MEIN RANT

A Summary in Light Verse of
"MEIN KAMPF"

BY

R. F. PATTERSON

Illustrated by

W. HEATH ROBINSON

"My desire is ... that mine adversary had written a book."
—*Job, xxxi, 35.*

WAVERLEY
BOOKS

First published by Blackie & Son Limited,
London and Glasgow
1940

This facsimile edition published
September 2009 by
Waverley Books,
David Dale House, New Lanark,
ML11 9DJ, Scotland

Illustrations by W. Heath Robinson,
© 2009 The Estate of Mrs J. C. Robinson
Text by Dr Richard Ferrar Patterson,
© 2009 The Gresham Publishing Partnership

ISBN 978 1 84934 002 1

Printed and bound in the EU

Publisher's Note:
About *Mein Rant*

Summer 2009

Mein Rant is a verse-satire of Hitler's *Mein Kampf*. Its author, Dr Richard Ferrar Patterson said of it: '*Mein Kampf* had neither rhyme nor reason, while my abridgement undoubtedly has rhyme.' *Mein Rant* was first published in February 1940, five months after the outbreak of war. Written by Dr Patterson, an editor at Blackie & Son publishers, which had offices in both Glasgow and London, the book was illustrated by Heath Robinson, who was a celebrated artist, and well known for his drawings of absurdly complicated inventions. It is noteworthy that *Mein Rant* was printed in Blackie & Son Glasgow print works, which by then had been given over to the war effort. The book was thus printed in between shifts of torpedo manufacture.

The spirit and humour of *Mein Rant* were very much of their time. During the Second World War, laughing in the face of danger at the German aggressors was a typical response from Britain's writers, cartoonists and editors. Hitler had a most-wanted list, with names of prominent newspaper editors and publishers, who, had Germany invaded the UK, were to be captured and made answerable for their crime of 'gross disrespect' to the Führer. The editor of *The Beano* comic was on this list, for example, as was comic artist Dudley Watkins. Watkins had been held back from active military service owing to the irreplaceable positive impact he was seen to be making on the nation's morale in *The Beano*. The British attitude was unique amongst the warring countries, in that it aimed to ridicule the opposition. German propaganda, on the other hand, was mostly malicious, especially in its portrayal of Jewish citizens. It showed them as people to be feared, and the Germans issued dire warnings of what would befall Germany if the Jewish people prospered.

Fighting back with indomitable humour – laughing at the enemy – took people's minds off the danger they faced. Propaganda, of course, works as an appeal to the emotions, rather than logic, but the British style of lampooning the Germans won both hearts and minds at home. By reducing the enemy to mocked idiots and clowns, the aggressors were less of a threatening and evil force, and satire shrunk the enemy down to size. The contrast with other nations' propaganda was stark. Italy, for example, banned all foreign comics, including *The Beano* and, indeed, America's Mickey Mouse.

Mein Kampf (*My Struggle*), Hitler's autobiography, was written while Hitler was in Landsberg Prison. Often incoherent, the book was written after Hitler's five-year sentence for taking part in the 1923 Beer Hall Putsch. He was treated generously in prison, and allowed to walk in the grounds, receive guests and read. It was here that he was encouraged to write his autobiography. Never keen on writing however, Hitler had his chauffeur, Emile Maurice, live in the prison and begin ghostwriting it for him. When that plan failed, Rudolf Hess, a student from Munich University who was imprisoned at the same time as Hitler for the Beer Hall Putsch, took up the task, and it is said, added his own notes to the manuscript.

Hitler outlined his views for the Aryan race in *Mein Kampf*. He believed that the Aryans should run the world and, with force, could do so. He wanted a 'lebensraum' (living space) in the East, as he believed that the Jewish race was in conspiracy with the Communists, and that the two had power over Russia. Hitler wanted Britain to help him defeat the Russians, who he believed would otherwise take over the rest of Europe. William L Shirer, an American journalist and historian, and one of the most recognized Americans to have visited Nazi Germany, said of Hitler, 'he never escaped from mental adolescence'.

Mein Kampf was published in two volumes

in 1926 and 1927. It went on to be published in three different editions while Hitler was in power from 1933–1945. Apart from the mass-market edition, with a picture of Hitler on the front and a swastika, there was a wedding-gift edition, and later an edition intended for a loved-one fighting at the front. The book was promoted as the essential volume for every German home.

Mein Rant – the satire of *Mein Kampf* – was published when Britain was struggling in the war against Germany. Today it may seem incredible to us that Britain entered the war with many expecting surrender to the Germans within a year. When Germany invaded Poland on 1 September 1939, to reclaim the land they 'lost' after the First World War, many feared that Britain would not honour her many pledges of support to Poland.

Britain stood alone. France, fearing another major war, stood aside and would not help Britain at that time; the USA was not prepared to get involved either. Suddenly Adolf Hitler, with whom Prime Minister Chamberlain had negotiated 'peace in our time', and whom Lord Halifax, the Conservative Foreign Secretary, had called 'most sincere', was revealed for what he was.

Within six months of declaring war, Britain faced massive losses and possible surrender. By May 1940, Prime Minister Winston Churchill was (secretly) being asked to approve plans to evacuate the Government, the Royal Family and the Bank of England's gold to Canada. Some 200,000 British troops stood on the beaches of Dunkirk, unable to get home, while Churchill bartered with the Americans to send destroyers to help rescue them. In the previous six months, children had been evacuated from London and other cities; men had been called up, and mobilised; and women had gone to work in munitions factories to do men's jobs for the first time. People knew their lives would never be the same again.

Indeed, by the end of the war, eleven million innocent people had died in Hitler's death camps, and the overall deaths of the Second World War are estimated to be between fifty and seventy million.

New Lanark
2009

Taken from the County Jail
   By a set of curious chances; . . .
Wafted by a favouring gale
   As one sometimes is in trances,
To a height that few can scale,
   Save by long and weary dances;
Surely never had a male
   Under such like circumstances
So adventurous a tale,
   Which may rank with most romances.

                    W. S. GILBERT, *The Mikado,* ACT I.

PREFACE

For many years a knowledge of Archdeacon Paley's *Evidences of Christianity* was essential in order to pass the Little-go at Cambridge. This book is somewhat formidable, I am told; I have never personally examined a copy. Even serious students at Cambridge contented themselves with mastering a small epitome of the book, tastefully bound in light blue paper and compiled by a former cox of the University boat. The more frivolous undergraduates, however, were able to satisfy the examiners by getting up a metrical version of the *Evidences*, which claimed to have been written by Paley's Ghost.

It has occurred to me that *Mein Kampf* might benefit by similar treatment, and that a metrical epitome of it might give the reader all he wants to know about the book in a more compressed and palatable form than the original text. Its talented author has learnt many lessons in his journey through life, but has not learnt that brevity is the soul of wit.

In one respect my epitome has the advantage

over the original; the book in its pristine state has neither rhyme nor reason, while my abridgment undoubtedly has rhyme.

R. F. P.

GLASGOW
February, 1940.

Messrs. Blackie and Son, Ltd., acknowledge their indebtedness to Miss Nancy McIntosh and to Messrs. Macmillan and Co., Ltd., for permission to reproduce the quotation from The Mikado *on p. v.*

AUTHOR'S PREFACE

Because I did a spell in prison
The ensuing volume has arisen;
I found my temporary fetters
Conducive to the craft of letters.

Here I've described, in prison pent,
My personal development,

xv

Reducing thus to nothingness
The inventions of the Jewish press.

My case especially I plead
With followers of the Nazi creed,
That those who think aright and soundly
May study it the more profoundly.

I know that written words are weaker
Than those of an accomplished speaker,
For every vacillating doubter
Is stung to action by a spouter.

Still, what is written, if it's sense,
Achieves a greater permanence;
And here I've written what you'll own
Is Nazidom's foundation stone.

A. H.

THE FORTRESS,
LANDSBERG AM LECH.

VOLUME I

A RETROSPECT

I. My Start

I'm Fortune's favourite from birth,
Because, of all the spots on earth,
'Twas Braunau Fate decreed should be
The scene of my nativity.

It's Austrian, you'll understand,
But yet upon the borderland;
I dreamt of *Anschluss* in my youth,
Before I cut my earliest tooth.

My father was a man deserving
Whose *métier* was civil serving;
He wished that I, for my vocation,
Should choose a similar occupation.

But not at all; though stout my nerve is,
It jibbed at thoughts of civil service;
And I decided that at least
I'd be an abbot or a priest.

But my respected parent said
" You're far too big a dunderhead."
And I replied in accents fainter
" Well then, I'd rather be a painter,"

" My soul with happiness o'ergushes
At thoughts of paint-pots and of brushes,
And naught on earth would make me gladder
Than climbing up and down a ladder.

" A painter and a decorator!
No human lot can e'er be greater."
So, filled with dreams of trestle-boards,
I made my way Viennawards.

4

II. Vienna

I underwent a course of cram,
And sat a most unfair exam;
For, though my genius cried aloud,
I ignominiously was ploughed.

[The examiner, the dirty dog,
Was member of a synagogue,
Or else, as I indeed surmise,
Was Mr. Churchill in disguise.]

Another walk of life selecting
I tried my hand at architecting
But found myself in a quandary,—
Some intellect was necessary.

And so, by dint of toil and slaving,
I satisfied my hunger's craving;
And thought myself most fortunate
In acting as a navvy's mate.

Ah me! what things I heard and saw;
I studied Nature in the raw,
And read, mid criminals and narks,
Das Kapital by Mister Marx.

I'd be as good as deaf and dumb
Had I not lived within a slum;
The source of all I shriek or mutter
Is that perennial fount, the gutter.

The Marxists wouldn't hesitate
To overturn the German state,
Or ruin Europe altogether
Their own Hebraic nests to feather.

From them I learnt the maxim trite
That Might invariably is Right;
That nothing disconcerts one's foes
Like hitting them upon the nose.

I learnt, moreover, that the throng
Abhors the weak and loves the strong,
And that a man, though vile and truthless,
Succeeds if he's completely ruthless.

I also learnt the curious news
That all our enemies are Jews,
That Destiny, when mischief *she* brews,
Has as her instrument the Hebrews.

My voice rose to a shrill falsetto
When speechifying on the Ghetto;
My words were full of sound and fury
When I denounced the crimes of Jewry.

6

I rose from this Serbonian bog
A most accomplished demagogue,
A man of most enlightened views,
A foe to Marxists and the Jews.

III. Reflections

Reflecting on the Austrian State
I saw that it was doomed by Fate;
'Twas absolutely misbegotten,
In all its inner workings rotten.

It was indeed, I made confession,
A geographical expression;
'Twas rickety and out of date,
Unworthy to be called a state.

I saw that Parliaments were vain,
And viewed them with complete disdain,
As gatherings of raucous rabble,
Mere devotees of gas and gabble.

In vain democracy supposes
That virtue lies in counting noses;
The ignorant, self-seeking throng
Is never right and always wrong,

But public life at once gets purer
'Neath the direction of a Fuehrer,
Provided he's like me, but then
I'm one of Nature's gentlemen.

Timidity and self-conceit
Soon make a populace effete,
And life is only truly thrilling
When spent in musketry and drilling.

And reason's only active when
Within the brains of common men;
In every fat diplomatist
It simply ceases to exist,

For he misleads the common herd
In fashion that is quite absurd;
They follow each Semitic viper
As Hamelin's children did the piper.

A People, you must understand,
· Does not, of course, connote a land;
For Jews, although devoid of acres,
Are universal mischief makers.

Yes, look wherever you may choose,
You'll find bad ha'pennies and Jews;
And commoner than fleas or ticks,
Are democrats and Bolsheviks.

I knelt and prayed to mighty Thor

V. The World War

I used to sit and curse my fate
Because I had been born too late;
In a commercial age a hero
Is worth but little more than zero.

By nature a determined Stoic
I panted after deeds heroic;
When Archduke Francis Ferdinand
Was liquidated, it was grand.

And when I learnt we were at war
I knelt and prayed to mighty Thor,
For I perceived I had a chance
Of freedom and deliverance.

Inspired by notions such as these
I learnt " Eyes Right " and " Stand at ease ",
I grew expert at marking time,
My forming fours was quite sublime.

I learnt, in my desire to fight,
The difference 'twixt Left and Right,
But never could remember long
The difference 'twixt Right and Wrong.

I loved my military appointment;
The only fly within the ointment
Was fear that, ere I saw a trench,
We should have finished with the French.

At last my training was completed,
Behold me now in troop-train seated;
Bedecked with boots and field-grey tunic
I left the friendly town of Munich.

Thanks to my prowess and my cunning
My job was regimental running,
It also was, a little later,
To act as regimental waiter.

With equally heroic mates
I washed up saucers, cups and plates;
With freedom's other gallant warders
I handed round battalion orders.

I took twelve Poilus single-handed,
And so the Iron Cross I landed,
At least I think I did; meseems
'Twas only in the Land of Dreams.

VI. War Propaganda

The common populace can stand a
Tremendous lot of propaganda,
Of course provided that the stuff
Is imbecile and base enough.

Our propaganda, sad to say,
Was managed in a futile way,
Whereas our foemen were expert
At flinging every kind of dirt.

Our foes excelled themselves, like ganders,
At hissing calumnies and slanders;
Our publicists were things of scorn,
As innocent as babes unborn.

For never, in or out of season,
Should propaganda aim at reason,
It should appeal to all that's base
And evil in the human race.

For all the lesser tribes and sects
Are feeble in their intellects,
And you can only rouse a nation
By damnable reiteration.

For this an adept is required
And that's the reason I have hired,
Whene'er my genius boils and burbles,
My mouthpiece, Dr. Joseph Goebbels.

A slogan should be shouted loud
Till people's intellects are cowed;
It should be shouted o'er and o'er,
For that's the way to win a war.

VII. The Revolution

The enemy's malicious cunning
Was more effective than his gunning,
His subtle snares and treacherous nets
Were deadlier than his bayonets.

His cool effrontery and aplomb
Were far more fatal than a bomb;
His propaganda slew more folks
Than guns of Maxim or of Stokes.

The womenfolk were much to blame
For Germany's defeat and shame;
The letters of our girls and wives
Cost thousands of our soldiers' lives;

For every closely-written sheet
Breathed forth the spirit of defeat;
It was defeatism, not tanks,
That broke our courage and our ranks.

Our armies never were defeated,—
They just strategically retreated;
It was the Hebraic, Marxist pack
That stabbed our soldiers in the back.

For just as victory was nigh
They raised a novel battle-cry
Of " Vote for each and votes for all ",
A sorry kind of trumpet call.

Instead of singing *Wacht am Rhein*,
These dissolute Judaic swine
Would sing, in trenches and in cities,
Their evil communistic ditties.

These Jews, I'll take my affydavy,
Corrupted all our gallant Navy,
Which, as it lay securely anchored,
With Red Sedition's germs was cankered.

With Jews and all their packs of lies
No upright man can compromise;
And so I launched, devoid of fear,
On a political career.

VIII. Political Activities

Three hang-dog fellows came to me
To take me into custody;
They shouted to me " Hands up now, sir,"
But didn't care to face my Mauser.

I said " We mustn't be down-hearted,"
And so another party started,
Designed to captivate those asses
The vulgar proletarian masses.

The superman (like me) who leads
Must plan far more than acts or deeds,
And ought to concentrate his soul
On nothing save his final goal.

The Leader with his boundless view
Plans more than mortal man can do;
Our Christian faith, though based on love,
Reflects but palely things above.

A Leader is no petty schemer,
He is a visionary and dreamer,
In all his mental lucubrations
He plans for future generations.

While ordinary men, I fear,
Think more of bread and beef and beer,
And how to spot a likely winner,
And what will be to-morrow's dinner.

But fortunately now and then
Is born a mighty man of men,
Who steers the Ship of State through storms
By means of radical reforms.

The thorny path of life grows smoother
When I reflect on Martin Luther,
And I contrive to feel less sick
When contemplating Frederick.

I soon found out my path to glory
Lay through incessant oratory;
And those who understood my lingo
Were charmed by words in praise of Jingo.

With vehemence I roared and shouted,
I shrieked, I ranted and I spouted,
I growled, I muttered and I hissed
Like any crude revivalist.

IX. The German Workers' Party

Orating more than other men did,
Full many a meeting I attended,
And I received a very hearty
Request to join the Workers' Party.

This was a small debating club
Assembling in a third-rate pub,
A building desolate and blighted,
Exceptionally badly lighted.

Its membership was almost nix,
Its funds were barely six-and-six,
Its correspondence somewhat thin—
Three letters out, three letters in.

I got a bad attack of hump
While they discussed the Parish Pump;
But yet, although of small dimensions,
They overflowed with good intentions.

This party, though 'twas undersized,
Was not, at present, fossilized;
Because its principles were lax
It might be mouldable like wax.

It seemed a trivial affair,
A blend of pathos and hot air;
Said I " I'll rouse it from its slumber ":—
I joined it; Seven was my number.

X. Why the Second Reich Collapsed

The Second Reich derived its charms
From all its glorious feats of arms,
For men invariably endorse
Whatever may be based on force.

But yet it showed, as clear as day,
The signs of premature decay,
And prescient far-seeing chaps
Were not surprised at its collapse.

Our difficulties came about
Through no mere military rout,
Because, as I've explained before,
We were not beaten in the war.

Nor were they due, you must confess,
To economic strain and stress,
They were indubitably due
To Nature's sole mistake, the Jew.

The statesman who is sage and wise
Will not indulge in petty lies,
For if he tells a mighty whopper
His conduct will be far more proper.

If mud is scattered good and thick
Why, some of it is sure to stick;
Mendacity will never fail
When practised on colossal scale.

Our Art displayed, to men of sense,
The clearest signs of decadence;
A prey to heresy and schism
It drifted into Futurism.

Our Literature was paralytic,
And most unwholesomely Semitic;
None of our literary pillars
Was Goethe's peer, or even Schiller's.

Our greatness, then, was due alone
To three things, third of them the Throne,
The Civil Service was the second,
The first the Army, as I've reckoned.

Though each its part serenely played
Still we inevitably decayed,
Because we paid, to our disgrace,
No thought to Problems of the Race.

Normally, kind mates with kind

XI. Race and People

Although myself a celibate
My biologic lore is great;
And somehow I contrived to find
That, normally, kind mates with kind.

'Tis one of Nature's changeless laws
That daws will only pair with daws;
Lion with lioness cohabits,
And rabbits only mate with rabbits.

Wrens fall in love with other wrens,
And cocks ally themselves with hens;
A mouse will only woo a fit mouse,
A titmouse courts another titmouse.

When Adam, in his lordly way,
The brute creation did survey,
He did not find a single brute
His matrimonial views to suit.

And yet our youths and maidens choose
For wives and husbands alien Jews,
And blood that's sound or even bluish
Degenerates when mixed with Jewish.

The Jews are everything that's base,
A filthy and an outcast race,
Whose language serves to cloak their thought,
Who've never worked and never fought.

What they consider a career
Is buying cheap and selling dear,
Or, what's enough to make one furious,
The loan of cash on terms usurious.

Their horrible transactions range
Through every nation's Stock Exchange;
They've sworn allegiance to those base 'uns,
The Order of Accepted Masons.

To get us in a dangerous mess
They've subsidized the German press,
And, as their last and chief resource,
They use that ugly weapon, Force.

Ignoble, too, in all their dealings
They flatter all our baser feelings,
And never show the least respect
As Nazis do, to intellect.

Consider, pray, the state of Russia
(Complete antithesis to Prussia),
Where Marxists rule, and Jewish scum
Makes every true progressive dumb.

A nation only will endure
Whose blood is absolutely pure;
One law our destiny determines,
That Germany must be for Germans.

XII. First Stage of Nazis

Just here I don't propose to retail
Our ideology in detail,
I shall require another ream
Of paper for so grand a theme.

Our movement's great foundation-stone
Is force, but is not force alone;
A Thug who's resolute can stifle
A cowardly fellow with a rifle.

Our movement therefore fosters hate
'Gainst other parties in the state,
For hatred's better far at striking
A deadly blow, than mere disliking.

A pug, although you pinch and nip it,
Can never emulate a whippet;
It will remain obese and sluggish,
And in its inmost nature puggish.

A leader, though with talent dowered,
Will not succeed if he's a coward;
A leader must be strong and bold,
And cast in an heroic mould.

Persuasively we kicked downstairs

The church's spiritual home
Has always been eternal Rome,
Carthage was hub of empire Punic,
Our spiritual centre's Munich.

We gladly underwent the hatred
Of those who'd paint the German state red;
The more the Jewish Press abused us
The more complacency suffused us.

Our meetings sparsely were attended,
But grew, ere long, to gatherings splendid;
Our enemies, caught unawares,
Persuasively we kicked downstairs.

It soon became as clear as day
A mighty Force was under way,
A Goddess bringing retribution
For our November revolution.

Our party never brooked a rival
In Germany's superb revival;
From every Communist intrigue freed
We forged anew the Sword of Siegfried.

VOLUME II

THE NAZI MOVEMENT

I. World Philosophy and Party

In Nazi history one traces
Its solid philosophical basis;
All other parties trust to lies
And oft-repeated parrot-cries.

The men who constitute our Senates
Are vacillating in their tenets,
And change, to satisfy the Grundies,
Their outlook oftener than their undies.

Our gallant fighting men determine
To change their shirts when full of vermin;
Our politicians, with like ease,
Discard unpopular policies.

The Marxists' policy is stuff,
It's based on nothing else but bluff,
They have, what's more, no sense of shame,
They don't attempt to play the game,

While we are full of good intents,
A lot of perfect little gents,
And I, the German nation's saviour,
Am noted for my good behaviour.

Philosophy, however right,
Must none the less be based on might,
And truths are vain unless one backs 'em
With knuckleduster, bomb and Maxim.

The Nazi system needs as Leader
An eloquent persuasive pleader,
To form its programme and to plan it
As firmly as a block of granite.

The Marxist doctrine is a lot
Of unadulterated rot;
Like rottenness it daily spreads
From silly heads to silly heads.

A master-race must come to birth
To lord it over all the earth,
And such a race can only be
The race which generated me.

Our system must derive its vigour
From its uncompromising rigour;
If we are to succeed, we must
Reduce our enemies to dust.

II. The State

A homogeneous race's token
Is not the language that is spoken;
A race is truly one whose veins
Are undefiled by foreign strains.

Yet, in the ignorant U.S.A.,
The immigration officers say,
Addressing one of Abraham's seed
" I guess you are of German breed ".

The mammoth and the dinosaur
And pterodactyl are no more;
In fashion similar will vanish
The French, the British, and the Spanish.

The earliest tribes of Aryans,
Were by no means barbarians,
Nay, as the Muse of History speaks,
We were the compeers of the Greeks.

Our country all the same is what
Might well be termed a melting pot,
A mass, as it appears to me,
Of heterogeneity.

Yet Germany could rule the earth
From Timbuctoo as far as Perth,
If but her blood were unalloyed
And not half man, half anthropoid.

With this in view the German nation
Requires a special education;
Our young Apollos should bear witness
To Germany's essential fitness.

Our old curriculum was vain,
Neglecting brawn and fostering brain;
It was superfluous, never doubt it—
Just see how I've got on without it.

Young man, if you will only train
Your body and neglect your brain,
You may become in course of time
As fine a specimen as I'm.

It is a perfect shame that Jews
Professional careers can choose,
While Aryans and other just men
Turn into scavengers and dustmen.

All men who work, whate'er their station,
Should get the same remuneration,
Whether they steer the Ship of State,
Or merely paint and decorate.

If we were not the slaves of Mammon
We'd call the present system gammon;
Our Nazi spirit will set free all
By cultivating the ideal.

III. Citizens and Subjects of the State

Our laws of naturalization
Are quite unworthy of our nation,
For they allow a Pole or Burman
Or Zulu to become a German.

A foreigner, if he's a cute 'un,
Can thus by law become a Teuton,
The law can germanize a Jew—
A thing the Almighty cannot do.

It's true we don't accept a plotter,
Or common footpad or garrotter,
But, short of that, our state embraces
A lot of alien disgraces.

To join a nation seems to be
Like joining some Society,
You pay a fee, fill in a slip,
And get a card of membership.

More regal than a foreign King

Men should as citizens be rated
Only when duly educated,
That is, of course, when they arrive at
The status of a full-blown private.

And when each conscientious plodder
Is qualified as cannon-fodder,
He ought to be acclaimed and fêted
And solemnly certificated.

No patriot would exchange this charter
Of civic rights for Star or Garter;
A German scavenger's a thing
More regal than a foreign King.

IV. Personality and the People's State

Now let me hasten to explain,
One brain excels another brain;
Some men are useless, save as breeders,
While others are cut out for Leaders.

Man first subdued the ox and horse,
Then, by judicious use of force,
He grew more powerful, and then
He subjugated other men.

The marvellous inventions which
Our daily modern life enrich,
Are one and all, I think you'll find,
The offspring of a single mind.

Hence it is absolutely plain
That Leaders must be men of brain,
Prepared to go to any length
To lead mankind from strength to strength.

41

They should be sacrosanct because
They can't be judged by normal laws,
In fact, to use a hackneyed phrase,
Their ways are not as others' ways.

The Marxists say a vulgar mob
Can do what is a Leader's job,
But they and others such as they
Are harbingers of vile decay.

Look at our army—look what *they* did!
All their authority is graded;
We Nazis in their steps must toddle,
We couldn't have a better model.

A major, in his course diurnal,
Must bow to a lieutenant-colonel;
A subaltern, though vastly sager,
Must click his heels before a major.

So, in our council chambers, less men
Must all become a herd of yes-men;
And everyone, of course, is littler
Than I, the Fuehrer, Adolf Hitler.

V. Organization

A necessary pre-condition
For building must be demolition;
The early Christians razed, as *you* know,
The shrines of Jupiter and Juno.

The early Christians found that terror's
The most effective cure for errors;
'Twas absolute intolerance
That made their sacred cause advance.

By posing as infallible
They made the people malleable;
We too must practise an extensive
And ruthlessly severe offensive.

The ordinary party man
Requires to know his Leader's plan
No more than rankers understand
Campaigns their general has planned.

The rank and file need not be skilled,
But must be thoroughly well drilled,
They have no need of any sense,
Their rôle is blind obedience.

Our programme must be fixed and not
Be altered in a single jot,
For any kind of variation
Is sure to cause disintegration.

Our programme won't succeed (how can it?)
Unless immutable as granite;
Our cure for ills of state must be a
Complete and perfect panacea.

I urge on you in my orations
To spurn all worthless imitations;
All other writers are mere hacks,
All other orators are quacks.

VI. The First Period of Our Struggle

In all my many speeches I
Denounced the Treaty of Versailles,
I also shouted o'er and o'er
We weren't responsible for war.

A public speaker or reciter
Is far more powerful than a writer,
For written statements can be checked
And criticized if incorrect.

And promises, if merely spoken,
Can more conveniently be broken,
While spoken lies, if unsuspected,
Are far less easily detected.

In their nefarious deeds and acts
The Marxists recognized these facts;
To spread their policy these crooks
Made use of speakers, not of books.

For then its mental powers are weaker
And less resistant to a speaker.

The people found each Marxist writing
Peculiarly uninviting,
But speakers won them in a trice
By promises of Paradise.

Remember, if you're timed to speak
At 10 a.m., use one technique;
You should adroitly change your tune
When speaking in the afternoon.

But if you'd lead a mob aright
Address it, if you can, at night,
For then its mental powers are weaker
And less resistant to a speaker.

The wise man ne'er will be forgetting
Each work of art demands a setting;
E'en Wagner's operas delight you
Far more when they are played *in situ*.

The Church for every sacred rite
Prefers a dim religious light,
It hides its doctrine's somewhat thin sense
By means of thuribles and incense.

When asses in a herd combine
They're more than ever asinine;
A herd of men together huddled
Can much more easily be muddled.

VII. The Conflict with the Red Forces

The meetings of each other sect
Were very much what you'd expect;
To hear their tone apologetic
Affected me like an emetic.

Their speakers said " You must excuse me;
A hearing you will not refuse me;"
They were so pompous and so boring
That half the audience soon was snoring.

The Reds, of course, dispersed these meetings
By means of threats and even beatings;
I saw that it would not be hard
To hoist them with their own petard.

I mobilized each hefty lout
And trained him as a chucker-out;
I told him he must do or die
To vindicate our liberty.

I felt the savage joy of battle

When heckled by these Marxist swine
I merely had to give a sign;
We never argued with them, but
We cracked them on the occiput.

As we possessed no standard *pro tem*,
I planned to make a tribal totem,
So tough a task was this, my brain
With difficulty stood the strain.

The net result is rather nice,
A banner with a strange device,
The Swastika, which bears the sense
Of Aryan pre-eminence.

The Marxists, with their usual cheating,
Swore they'd disband our Monster Meeting;
I ordered all my trusty yeomen
To deal severely with the foemen.

When we attacked them at close quarters
The beer-mugs flew like Stokes's mortars;
The heads of all my trusty crowd
Were sanguinary, but unbowed.

'Mid pandemonium and rattle
I felt the savage joy of battle;
The ruffians for our gore who thirsted
Were most emphatically worsted.

VIII. The Strong is Strongest when Alone

There are innumerable movements
Which aim at national improvements,
And superficial thinkers claim
That all are virtually the same.

It's obvious to the thickest noddle
That this is nothing short of twaddle,
For Truth and Falsehood never mingle—
The Truth and I alike are single.

Though half-a-dozen crazy schemers
May pose as Germany's redeemers,
One man alone as gold is rated,
The others are electroplated.

Most leaders lose their high position
Through envy, malice or ambition,
Or bullying their weaker brothers,
Or taking what belongs to others.

It is superfluous to say
I don't behave that kind of way;
I keep my baser passions under,
I never give a thought to plunder.

These others, in their platform preachings,
Attempted to annex my teachings,
Though much that you will find therein
Is just about as old as sin.

The straightest pathway to perdition
Is to be found in coalition;
A coalition always suffers
From leadership of hopeless duffers.

The Real Leader, if he's wise,
Admits no kind of compromise,
For Nature only keeps alive
Those who are fittest to survive.

IX. Nature and Organization of Storm Troops

The Revolution, then, was due
To all the base civilian crew,
Though some civilians, I must say,
Were masquerading in field-grey.

When soldiers were no longer shot
For cowardice, they went to pot;
There's nothing like a firing-squad
For slackers who require a prod.

The Marxist leaders all were guys
Of elephantine bulk and size,
They were disgustingly obese,
Mountains of ugliness and grease.

You must confess there's not a German
That's half so svelte as Goering (Hermann);
And each of us you'll freely own is
A regular out-and-out Adonis.

The politician who succeeds
Will wisely mingle thoughts and deeds,
And he who'd conquer in a tussle
Must base his policy on muscle.

The Storm Troops (as I named this section)
Were organized for our protection,
But then, you see, to men of sense,
Attacking is the best defence.

One's foes most easily are sat on
By means of rubber cosh and baton;
For dealing with a gang of roughs
No method equals fisticuffs.

These Troopers were no secret corps,
Because, as I'd found out before,
The Germans have a fatal habit—
If there's a secret, they will blab it.

A ruffian's only routed fully
When up against a greater bully;
My Troopers' favourite cure for schism
Was unrestricted terrorism.

To do their duty then I bade them,
In handsome uniforms I clad them;
This garb distinguished Nazi Troopers
From ordinary vulgar snoopers.

And each of us you'll freely own is
A regular out-and-out Adonis.

X. The Mask of Federalism

The half-baked democratic pack
Lays all our woes on Prussia's back;
Our miseries, in truth, ensue
From not abolishing the Jew.

This nasty negroid parasite
Affects the Fatherland like blight,
And, in or out of marriage bonds,
Corrupts our guileless platinum blondes.

The Jew devotes his worthless life
To fostering internecine strife;
He likes those Protestants who vaunt if
They irritate the Roman pontiff.

The present Government behaves
Exactly like a gang of slaves,
But, though its conduct makes us fret so,
It's nothing but an intermezzo.

Confederacy, on the whole,
Has played a civilizing rôle,
But it should practise moderation,
And not too much centralization.

The lamps should still continue burning
In local shrines of light and learning,
For every celebrated place is
A kind of spiritual oasis.

The Army should, if well advised,
Be absolutely centralized,
Yet every new recruit should see
The length and breadth of Germany.

The Württemberger ought to feel
Completely at his ease at Kiel;
The Prussian, for his training area,
Should choose, if possible, Bavaria.

XI. Propaganda and Organization

Occasionally it may chance
A man of insignificance,
The butt of universal scorn,
May prove to be a Leader born.

A Propagandist ought to know
The human race is mean and low;
He should not fail to bear in mind
That it is cowardly and blind.

A Propagandist wakens numbers
Out of their gross, plebeian slumbers;
The Organizer's task's no lighter,—
From every score he picks a fighter.

Just now and then we light upon
That curious phenomenon,
A man both realist and dreamer—
And such am I, your true redeemer.

Within our Party's inner working
Some democratic germs were lurking;
We trusted still, the more's the pity,
The virtues of the sub-committee.

My caveat 'gainst this I entered,
All powers in myself I centred;
Peremptory as any Prussian
I did away with all discussion.

Our Party, being better nourished,
Like the proverbial bay-tree flourished;
Our money-matters grew far sounder,
We ceased in slough of debt to flounder.

We ran a paper of our own,
We soon acquired a telephone,
Electric light, a safe—in fact
No necessary thing we lacked.

Our rising fortunes made each critic
Completely dumb and paralytic;
We saved ourselves, at any rate,
A lot of tedious debate.

XII. The Problem of the Trade Unions

Trade Unions are, it seems to me,
An absolute necessity,
Although in this and other lands
They are controlled by Marxist hands.

Our system must, if we are wise,
Be founded on realities;
We are not like magicians that
Produce a rabbit from a hat.

The Unions should not foster strife
But guide our economic life;
Their duty is to see employment
Provides each worker with enjoyment.

The employer, too, should understand
That Joy and Work go hand in hand;
In every species of exertion
Freedom is better than coercion.

We Nazis seek our own survival,
We brook no sort or kind of rival,
And so we absolutely bar
Trade Unions as just now they are.

But Union members, as you know,
Expect to have a *quid pro quo*,
And, when we lift our coffers' lids,
We find a scarcity of quids.

We can't afford, ourselves alone,
To run a Union of our own;
So we must try another tack,
And stab our foemen in the back.

We'll overthrow, by infiltration,
The present-day organization;
By subtle subterranean schism
We'll bring about a cataclysm.

XIII. The German Post-War Policy of Alliances

Before we look across our border
We first must put our house in order;
To rehabilitate our pride
All means are fully justified.

Mere protestations won't restore
The glory that was ours of yore;
Discussion will not make us greater,
The Sword must be the arbitrator.

The British view with jaundiced eye
The growing French hegemony;
With Britain, for our private ends,
We must at any cost make friends.

To Britain's heart we must lay siege
If we'd regain our lost prestige;
When she's surrendered to our charms
We can with safety take up arms.

Will she be friends? Will she refuse?
Her Press is over-run with Jews,
Who overwhelm us with vile scandals,
And call us criminals and vandals.

The British Lion receiving orders

Small wonder every Briton shuns
The people whom he knows as Huns,
Especially our statesmen craven,
Who ignominiously did cave in.

If British friendship we should lose
The fault will be, of course, the Jews',
For everywhere the Hebrews go
Clandestinely they run the show.

The Jew would like to be a despot
From South America to Mespot;
The King of Beasts, the British Lion,
Receives his orders from Mount Zion.

XIV. Germany's Policy in Eastern Europe

The first essential for our race
Is amplitude of living space,
Which, if we have a grain of sense,
We'll get at Russia's sole expense.

The other Powers in land abound,
They have a lot of spreading ground;
While we are worse than what's deplored
By a Congested Districts Board.

The human species has progressed
From bad to good and then to best;
The richest and the rarest fruit on
The Tree of Progress is the Teuton.

A dozen colonies will not
At all alleviate our lot,
New European territory
Is Germany's sole path to glory.

The other nations must be minions
O'ershadowed by our Eagle's pinions;
We must possess the earth entire
Or else immediately expire.

Red Russia is an institution
Entirely ripe for dissolution;
We're destined, when her empire ceases,
To gather up the broken pieces.

Her folk are cruel and rapacious,
And most incredibly mendacious,
Yes, search the world till kingdom come,
You'll never find a fouler scum.

If they allied themselves with us
They'd prove a fatal incubus;
The only weapons they devise
Are lies and lies and yet more lies.

The Russian is a savage brute
Who gloats on murder and on loot,
With every nameless stigma branded,
Degraded, bestial, bloody-handed.

Were he our ally it would be
Inevitable catastrophe;
His doom would be the Germans' doom,
His tomb would be the Germans' tomb.

XV. The Right to Self-defence

The enemy destroyed our nation
By slow persistent strangulation,
An operation which, if slow,
Is all the surer being so.

Our leaders were a lot of dastards,
And semi-oriental bastards;
No wonder that their gait was hobbling,
They came from glove-making and cobbling.

Of course there is no kind of taint
Attached to putty or to paint;
A trade's a noble thing, provided
You practise it as well as I did.

I much admire the ancient Dago
Who said " Delenda est Carthago ";
We must destroy, once and for all,
The empire and the might of Gaul.

When Frenchmen occupied the Ruhr
To make their own position sure,
Then was the time to strike a blow
To pulverize our Gallic foe.

We could not have attacked, of course,
But should have made a show of force;
We could have carried out the bluff
If we'd been organized enough.

But in and out of every season
Our Marxists wallow in high treason;
Like dogs returning to their vomit,
You cannot separate them from it.

When planning how to get their scalps
I cast my eyes beyond the Alps,
Where the heroical Benito
Has put on Communists a veto.

When Jews and Communists are scattered
Our nation's fetters will be shattered;
We'll slay the traitors in our camp,
And then re-kindle Freedom's lamp.

Yes!   Clio, History's own Muse,
Will give us mighty men our dues;
Although to prison you remit us,
The Muse of History will acquit us.

Envoi

Behold the volume I have writ,
A masterpiece of style and wit;
I make my soldiers carry it,
Like iron rations, in their kit.

O readers, who have read, in rhyme,
My gallant deeds, my thoughts sublime,
You'll all agree with me that I'm
The greatest German of all time.